TWISTS AND TURNS

FORCES IN MOTION

By Nathan Lepora

Consultant: Suzy Gazlay, M.A.,
science curriculum resource teacher

Gareth Stevens
Publishing

Please visit our web site at www.garethstevens.com.
For a free catalog describing our list of high-quality books, call 1-800-542-2595 (USA)
or 1-800-387-3178 (Canada). Our fax: 1-877-542-2596

Library of Congress Cataloging-in-Publication Data
Lepora, Nathan.
    Twists and turns : forces in motion / Nathan Lepora.
      p. cm. – (The science behind thrill rides)
    Includes index.
    ISBN-10: 0-8368-8945-2 ISBN-13: 978-0-8368-8945-1 (lib. bdg.)
    ISBN-10: 0-8368-8950-9 ISBN-13: 978-0-8368-8950-5 (softcover)
    1. Rotational motion—Juvenile literature. 2. Force and
energy—Juvenile literature. I. Title.
    QC133.5.L47 2008
    531'.3—dc22   2007042002

This North American edition first published in 2008 by
Gareth Stevens Publishing
A Weekly Reader® Company
1 Reader's Digest Road
Pleasantville, NY 10570-7000 USA

This U.S. edition copyright © 2008 by Gareth Stevens, Inc. Original edition copyright © 2007 by ticktock Media Ltd.
First published in Great Britain in 2007 by ticktock Media Ltd., Unit 2, Orchard Business Centre, North Farm Road,
Tunbridge Wells, Kent, TN2 3XF United Kingdom

ticktock Project Editor: Sophie Furse
ticktock Picture Researcher: Lizzie Knowles
ticktock Project Designer: Hayley Terry
With thanks to: Carol Ryback, Justin Spain, Joe Harris

Gareth Stevens Editor: Jayne Keedle
Gareth Stevens Creative Director: Lisa Donovan
Gareth Stevens Graphic Designer: Farimah Toosi

Picture credits (t = top; b = bottom; c = center; l = left; r = right):
Howard Sayer/Alamy: cover. Richard Bannister: 26. DreamWorld/Ride Trade Int.Corp.Est: 28. Rod Edwards/Alamy: 9.
iStockphoto: 22. Caroline Johnson/Alamy: 4. Jupiter Images: 18–19 main. Kim Karpeles/Alamy: 29b. Lake County
Museum/Corbis: 19 inset. Mellor Images/Alamy: 12. Photolibrary Group: title page. Joseph Rehanek: 25 inset. Howard
Sayer/Alamy: 20 inset. Shutterstock: 6b, 17, 20–21 main, 23. Superstock: 14–15 main. Kumar Sriskandan/Alamy: 27.
Trip/Alamy: 5. David Wall/Alamy: 7. WizData, Inc./Alamy: 3. Colin Woodbridge/Alamy: 13. www.coasterimage.com: 11.
www.ultimaterollercoaster.com: 24–25 main.

Every effort has been made to trace copyright holders, and we apologize in advance for any omissions. We would be
pleased to insert the appropriate acknowledgments in any subsequent edition of this publication.

Printed in the United States of America

1 2 3 4 5 6 7 8 9 10 09 08 07

CONTENTS

CHAPTER 1: ROTATIONAL MOVEMENT

Roller coasters zoom around corners and swoop through loops. Carousels and Ferris wheels spin around a central point. Their circular movements are examples of **rotational movement.**

TERRIFYING TURNS

Roller coaster tracks use twists, sharp corners, and loops to thrill riders. Roller coaster cars zoom from side to side and swoop up and drop down. The cars have rotational movement as they thunder through each terrifying turn.

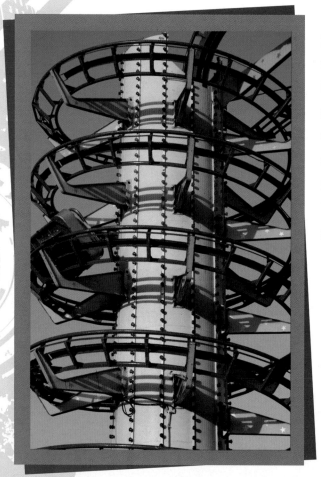

SENSATIONAL SPINS

Carousels and flying swings act like giant **spinning** wheels. You sit on the outside edges of the wheel and rotate around its center. As the wheel spins faster, rotational movement increases. The faster the spin, the more dizzy you feel.

LOOPY LOOPS

Sections of roller coasters called **loop-the-loops** turn the cars upside down. As you roar through the loops, you whoosh up, flip over, and zoom back down again. Each loop, turn, or twist causes rotational movement.

For many riders, the most thrilling moment is when they are upside down.

THAT'S AMAZING!

Inside your inner ear are tiny tubes filled with fluid. On a roller coaster ride, that fluid shifts and swirls, which makes you feel dizzy.

AXIS OF ROTATION

Imagine a rotating wheel. The wheel turns around an **axle,** a rod that runs through its center. An axle provides a fixed line to turn around. It is called the **axis of rotation**. The wheel spins on this line.

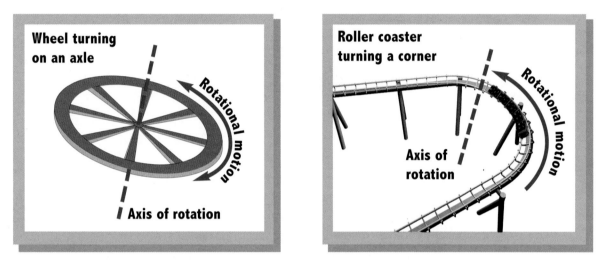

A wheel turning and a roller coaster going around a curve are two examples of rotational motion. Both turn around an axis.

ROTATING ROLLER COASTERS

A looping or turning roller coaster car has a different axis of rotation on each turn. Each curving section of track is shaped like part of a circle. The car rotates around a central axis through the middle of each circle.

THAT'S AMAZING!

Even the spinning Earth has an axis of rotation. Earth's axis of rotation is an imaginary line that goes through the planet from the north pole to the south pole.

INVISIBLE AXES

Most of the time, you cannot see the axes of a roller coaster. Instead, the axes are the invisible turning points for that ride. Think of the axes as imaginary centers for each turn, twist, or loop-the-loop.

The axis of rotation on this corkscrew roller coaster points through the middle of the loops (toward the two distant trees).

CHAPTER 2: ROTATIONAL ENERGY

Rotating objects have **energy** from turning or spinning around. This **rotational energy** helps carousels, roller coasters, and swings work.

WHAT IS ROTATIONAL ENERGY?

Energy makes things work. An object without energy is unable to do anything. There are many different forms of energy. Objects that turn or spin have rotational energy. The faster an object turns, the more rotational energy it has.

Velocity is the **speed** at which an object moves in a certain direction. A change in direction changes velocity. The rate at which an object's velocity changes over time is called **acceleration**.

THAT'S AMAZING

Carousels were invented about 1,500 years ago for practicing sword fighting while on horseback.

OTHER FORMS OF ENERGY

Kinetic energy and **potential energy** are two other types of energy. Moving objects have kinetic energy. An object about to fall has potential energy or stored energy. Potential energy changes into kinetic energy as the object falls.

Carousels have huge motors to provide the energy needed to spin them round and round.

ROTATIONAL ENERGY OF A ROLLER COASTER

Rotational energy is similar to kinetic energy because both energies come from movement. However, kinetic energy causes movement only in a straight line. Rotational energy is produced by turning a corner or spinning around.

The energy of a roller coaster changes during different parts of the ride. A roller coaster car at the top of a hill has potential energy. As the car travels downhill in a straight line, its potential energy becomes kinetic energy. When a roller coaster car turns a corner, its kinetic energy becomes rotational energy.

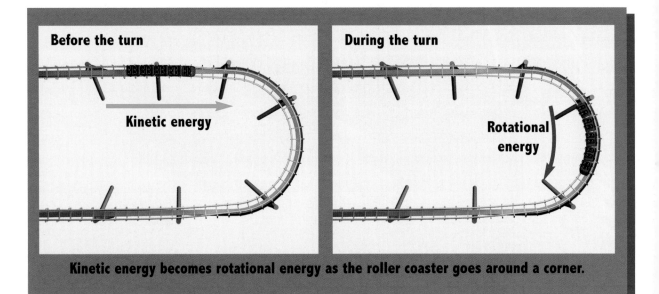

Before the turn

Kinetic energy

During the turn

Rotational energy

Kinetic energy becomes rotational energy as the roller coaster goes around a corner.

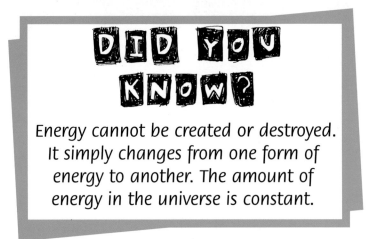

DID YOU KNOW?

Energy cannot be created or destroyed. It simply changes from one form of energy to another. The amount of energy in the universe is constant.

ROTATIONAL ENERGY OF A SWING

A swing at its highest point has potential energy. The swing falls with a circular motion. As it falls, it has both kinetic and rotational energy. **Gravity** causes the swing to accelerate as it goes down.

The Aero 360 swing ride at Kennywood in West Mifflin, Pennsylvania, spins vertically (up and down).

CHAPTER 3: CENTRIPETAL FORCE

A roller coaster car swerves around a corner. You feel like you and the car are being pushed to the outer edge of the track. However, a **force** is actually pushing the car in toward the axis of rotation. It is called the **centripetal force**.

WHAT IS CENTRIPETAL FORCE?

Any object that is turning has a centripetal force acting on it. This force causes moving objects to follow turns, corners, or loops. Without this centripetal force, the object could only move in a straight line. Centripetal force acting on a roller coaster comes from the tracks pushing on the cars.

Centripetal forces keep motorcycles
on a wall of death.

With every twist and turn, tracks push against the side of the wheels. That force changes the car's direction.

Going through a turn, riders feel pressed up against the side of the seat. The centripetal forces keep the cars on the tracks at every corner.

DID YOU KNOW?

Centripetal forces act at a right angle to the direction of movement. As the roller coaster speeds forward through a twist, you feel strong sideways forces.

Nemesis at Alton Towers in the United Kingdom allows riders' legs to swing free as they zoom around the twists and turns of the track.

HOW TO IMAGINE CENTRIPETAL FORCES

Imagine swinging a yo-yo around your head. You feel the yo-yo pulling against the string as it loops around. A centripetal force pulls along the string to make the yo-yo go around in a circle. Think of the string as the centripetal force in action.

If you let go of the string, the centripetal force disappears. Without the centripetal force, the yo-yo shoots off in a straight line.

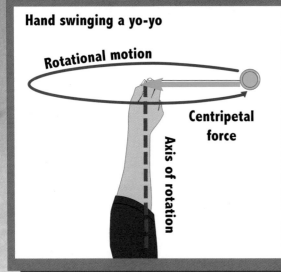

Hand swinging a yo-yo

Rotational motion

Centripetal force

Axis of rotation

The centripetal force is along the chains holding the seats on this ride.

NO STRINGS ATTACHED

Like the yo-yo, a swing ride has centripetal forces pulling along chains as it spins around. Centripetal force keeps the swings from flying off. Of course, roller coaster cars are not attached to strings. Instead, the curving tracks create the centripetal forces that push against the cars as they go around corners.

DID YOU KNOW?

Centri means 'center' and **petal** means 'toward' in Latin. A centripetal force pulls you toward the center of a turn.

CHAPTER 4: CORNERING

Swerving around corners is exciting on a roller coaster. Centripetal forces pull riders from one side of the car to the next, depending on which way the corner turns.

CRAZY CORNERS

When a roller coaster car turns left, its axis of rotation is also on the left. The car rotates around that axis as it swerves through a corner. The axis of rotation is different in each corner.

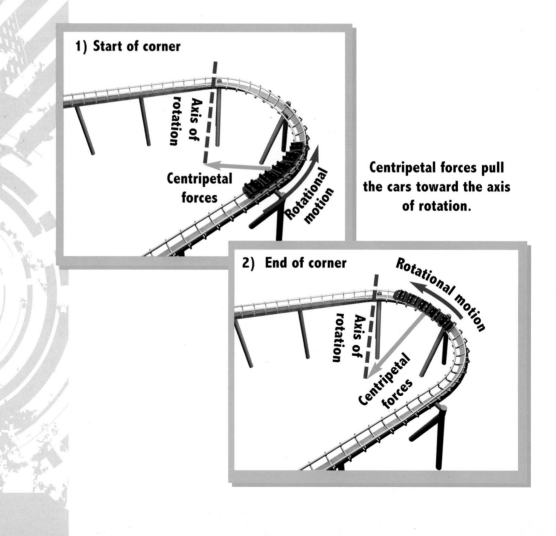

1) Start of corner

Axis of rotation

Centripetal forces

Rotational motion

Centripetal forces pull the cars toward the axis of rotation.

2) End of corner

Rotational motion

Axis of rotation

Centripetal forces

BANKED TRACKS

Roller coaster designers often build in a tilt or **bank** around a corner. The tracks are located at an angle to the axis of rotation. The centripetal force pushes into the tracks instead of across them. That keeps the sideways forces from pushing the cars off the tracks!

THAT'S AMAZING!

If you did not have safety bars on a roller coaster, turning a corner could throw you from the car!

The tracks on this roller coaster are tilted so that the cars will better turn the corner.

CHAPTER 5: LOOPING

Loop-the-loops are fun because they flip you upside down. Centripetal forces work with the forces of gravity and acceleration to keep you in the car.

LOOP-THE-LOOPS

Roller coaster cars enter a loop-the-loop at high speed. Rotational movement and the force of acceleration propels you through the loop. Centripetal forces pull the cars toward the loop-the-loop's axis of rotation.

DID YOU KNOW?

Flip-flap at Coney Island in New York, was the first U.S. roller coaster with a loop-the-loop. It was built in 1895 but closed in 1903 because of injuries to its riders. It is no longer standing.

Although they are very exciting, modern loop-the-loops are designed to be safe.

Early loop-the-loops had a circular shape.

OLD AND MODERN LOOPS

Early loop-the-loops had a very circular shape. That design created strong centripetal forces. Unfortunately, it also caused neck injuries by whipping riders' heads around too quickly.

Modern loop-the-loops have a special teardrop shape called a **clothoid** curve. The clothoid is a curving design that turns less tightly at its base to lessen the forces felt by riders.

HOW DO LOOP-THE-LOOPS WORK?

Gravity always pulls objects toward the ground.
When you flip over an egg carton, the eggs fall out
and splatter all over the floor. So why don't
you fall out of a roller coaster?

An object in motion wants to stay in
motion. So a roller coaster car
accelerating through a loop wants to keep
moving forward even as it moves up.

When you are upside down at the
top of the loop, gravity starts to
pull you toward the ground.
The force of acceleration
(and a safety harness)
keeps you in your seat.

THAT'S AMAZING!

Colossus at Thorpe Park in
Chertsey, England, holds the
record for the most loops.
It has a dizzying ten loops!

CENTRIPETAL FORCES AND GRAVITY

On a loop-the-loop you can also think of gravity supplying the centripetal force. Near the top of the loop, gravity provides the force that turns both you and the car around the loop!

At the start of a loop-the-loop the centripetal force points upward. This force turns the car up toward the sky.

Start of loop-the-loop

Centripetal forces

Rotational motion

At the top of a loop-the-loop the centripetal force points down.

Top of loop-the-loop

Rotational motion

Centripetal forces

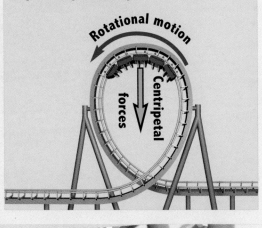

CHAPTER 6: SPINNING

Theme parks have many spinning rides, such as merry-go-rounds (carousels), flying swings, and Ferris wheels. Each spinning ride turns around an axis of rotation.

SPINNING RIDES

Unlike roller coasters, carousels and other spinning rides have a fixed axis of rotation. Riders whirl around one, stationary axis in a dizzying spin.

Riders enjoy the forces on a modern swing carousel ride.

The London Eye is the most popular tourist attraction in the United Kingdom.

TURNING FORCES

Huge motors power spinning rides. The motors provide the **turning force** that makes the ride begin to spin or rotate. The ride keeps rotating until brakes slow it down.

Turning forces differ from centripetal forces. Centripetal forces pull toward the axis of rotation at the center to keep an object turning. Turning forces work along the outside edges of an object and change the speed of rotation.

THAT'S AMAZING!

The London Eye spins at 0.6 miles (0.9 km) per hour which allows passengers to step on and off without the wheel needing to stop.

INTO THE FOURTH DIMENSION

Fourth-dimensional roller coasters are great fun. Riders sit on either side of the track in seats joined to long arms. The arms rotate freely during the ride to flip the seats forward or backward.

The roller coaster X in Valencia, California, was the world's first fourth-dimensional roller coaster. The ride starts with the seats tilting you headfirst down a twenty-story drop. Then you hurtle through a dizzying series of twists, flips, and loops!

The fourth-dimensional roller coaster X at Valencia, California

SPINNING ROLLER COASTERS

Some roller coasters cars can spin while zooming along. A common type of spinning roller coaster is called a crazy mouse. The bottom of each car rolls along the tracks while its upper part spins around.

A crazy mouse roller coaster at Grand Island, New York

THAT'S AMAZING!

The fourth-dimensional roller coaster Eejanaika in Fujiyoshida, Japan, flips its riders through 14 somersaults!

CHAPTER 7: SWINGS AND PENDULUMS

Another popular theme park ride has huge swings that whoosh forward and back. The swings move with a kind of rotational movement. After each swoop of their flight, the direction of rotation changes.

SCREAMING SWINGS AND PIRATE SHIPS

A theme park swing ride is a large version of a children's swing. Swing riders sit in suspended seats. The ride makes the swings move up and down as they swoop in and out.

Pirate ship rides are another popular theme park ride. These rides feature one or two open-seated ships attached to a long arm. The arm swings back-and-forth from a **pivot** point, through which the axis of rotation passes.

The Gauntlet is a screaming swing ride at Wild Adventures, Cypress Gardens, Florida.

WHAT IS A PENDULUM?

Swings and pirate rides act like giant **pendulums**. A pendulum is an object that hangs and swings freely from a fixed turning point called a pivot. If you pull a pendulum to one side and let it go, it swings back and forth until it runs out of energy.

The pirate ship ride, Santa Cruz Boardwalk, California

THAT'S AMAZING

The pirate ship ride was invented by Charles Albert Marshall of Oklahoma, between 1893 and 1897. He originally called it the Ocean Wave.

HOW DO PENDULUMS WORK?

A playground swing is a simple pendulum. The seat is the **weight** at the end of a rope that swings back and forth. It travels along a curved path.

With each pendulum movement, the swing seat drops down, then rises back up. The seat passes through its lowest point in the middle of each swing. At the outside of each swing, it reaches the highest point.

DID YOU KNOW?

The length of the pendulum determines how far the pirate ship ride will swing. The size of the ship doesn't matter.

The Claw, in Dreamworld, Australia, is the most powerful pendulum on the planet. Here it is at its highest point.

A swing seat moves because of gravity. As the swing seat falls, it accelerates. At the bottom of the swing, it is moving the fastest. It is also moving sideways. The speed carries the seat back up in the opposite direction, ready for its next swing back down.

HOW IT WORKS

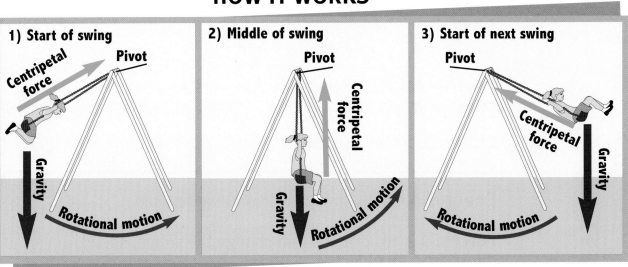

At the start of the swing, centripetal force pulls the swing seat in the direction of the pivot. At the same time gravity pulls it down. The swing seat drops down through the middle of its swing and rises back up again. It is then ready for centripetal force and gravity to pull it backwards on the next swing.

GLOSSARY

Acceleration: a change in speed or direction; an object speeding up is said to accelerate

Axle: the central rod around which a wheel turns

Axis of rotation: the line along which an object rotates. (The plural of axis is axes.)

Bank: a tilt along a track or course that improves a car's stability as it goes around a corner

Centripetal force: the force that pulls an object toward the center as it travels in a circle

Clothoid: a teardrop shape used for loop-the-loops on roller coasters to reduce the centripetal forces felt by riders

Energy: the ability to make something happen

Forces: pushes or pulls that change the shape, speed, or direction of an object

Gravity: a force of attraction between objects; gravity pulls objects toward Earth

Kinetic energy: a type of energy from movement

Loop-the-loop: a section of a roller coaster ride that sends its passengers looping up into the air, turning upside down, and looping back down again

Pendulum: an object hanging from a pivot that can rotate or swing freely

Pivot: a point around which an object turns

Potential energy: a type of energy that is stored

Rotational energy: energy from rotational (turning) movements

Rotational movement: a movement that turns an object. Cornering and spinning are two types of rotational movement.

Speed: how fast an object moves

Spinning: a type of rotational movement where an object turns around an axis of rotation that is centered within the object itself

Turning force: a force that causes an object to change its speed of rotation

Velocity: a measure of an object's speed in a particular direction

Weight: the pull of gravity on an object's mass

INDEX